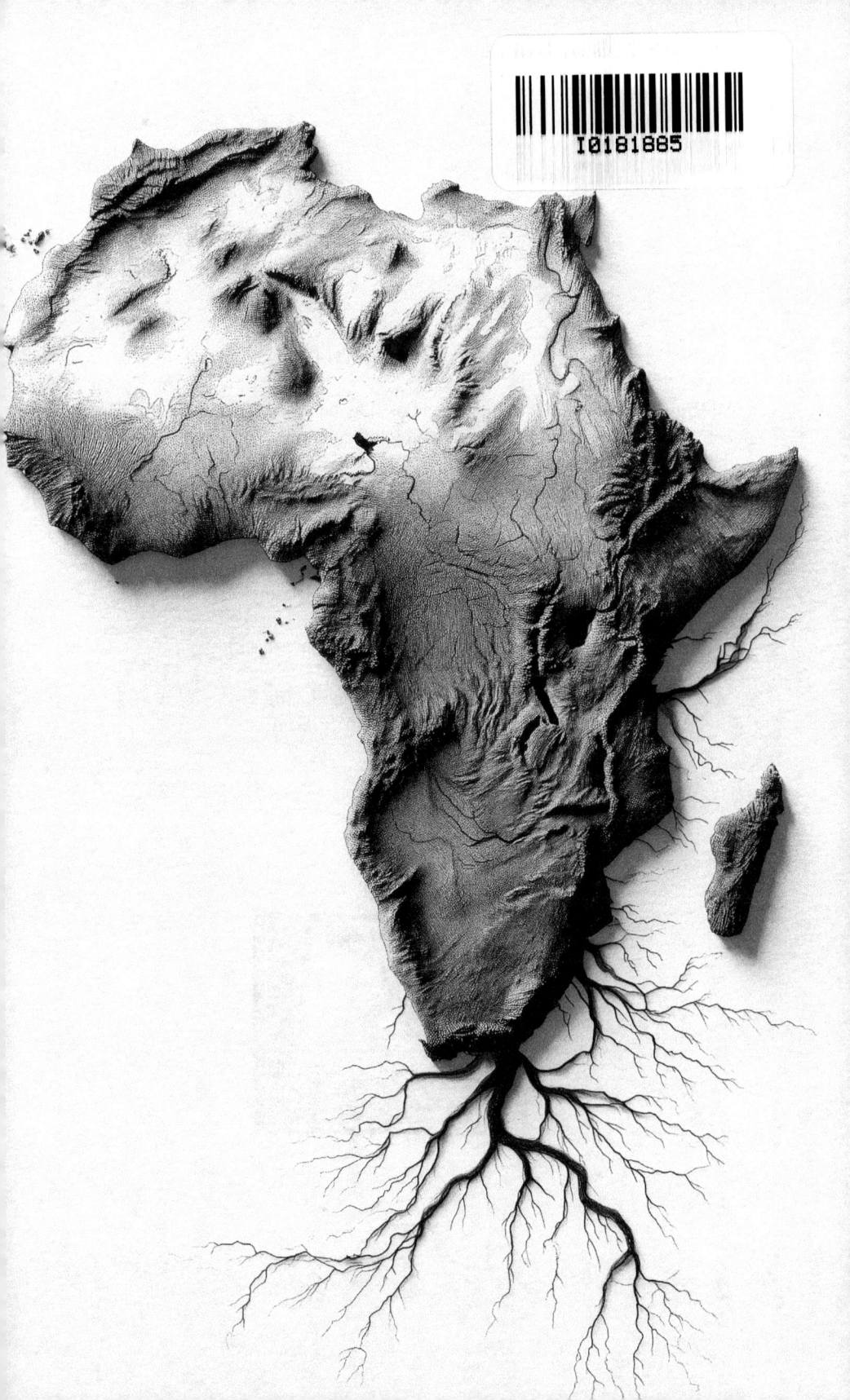

Copyright ©2025 by ATU Publishing

All Rights Reserved. No part of this book may be reproduced in any form or by an electronic or mechanical means, including information storage and retrieval systems, without permission in writing from the publisher, except by a reviewer who may quote brief passages in a review.

First Edition November 2025
Book Design by Kimberly Headley
Digital Art by Kimberly Headley

ISBN 979-8-9985966-1-2 (paperback)

Published by ATU Publishing
www.atupublishing.com

Akyiba
The Return

A collection

By Robert Coles

Editor's Note

Woven through centuries of conversation across time and space, this collection asks the reader to embrace the ephemerality of human experience while also understanding the permanence of its memory. Exploring identity, pearl-like in its constant defense against intrusions from the outside world, we are asked to reckon with the often overwhelming power the observer wields.

Touching on themes universal to the diasporic experience, this collection is at the same time also deeply personal. Each poem challenges the reader to both live in the moment while also observing it from afar. They are echoes back and forth across the Atlantic ocean, engaging the reader in what feels like an atemporal game of pingpong.

The title and section headings are borrowed from Twi, one of the major language families spoken in central and southern Ghana. This intentional choice on the part of the editor was made in an effort to ground the collection in a geographic center with great historical significance to the African Diaspora.

The artwork that appears alongside each poem serves to provide a visual extension to the written word. It has been an honor to bring this collection together and I am humbled to have been tasked with that undertaking.

Kimberly Headley

ACKNOWLEDGEMENTS

"Two Rivers" was published in MUDFISH, 2025

"So Many Things Divide Us" was published in PERSONALITIES (chapbook) by The Moonstone Arts Center, 2024

"Authentic African" was published in PERSONALITIES, 2024

"Harlem Hospital Waiting Room" was published by THE MACGUFFIN (Honorable Mention in the National Hunt Poetry Contest), vol. XIV, 1997

"Port Maria" was published in PERSONALITIES, 2024

"Runaways" was published in PERSONALITIES, 2024

"I Was Brown, They Were Black" was published in THE MINNESOTA REVIEW, #47, fall 1996

"The War Is Over" was published in PAINTBRUSH, 2000/2001

"Lost Memory" was published in MUDFISH, vol 14, 2005

"Red South" was published in PURSUING ALEXANDER PUSHKIN by Africa World Press, 2025

"Foreigner" was published in OBSIDIAN III, winter 1993-94

"In Sweden" was published in DESCANT, fall 1996

"African Museum" was published in THE EVANSVILLE REVIEW, vol. IX, spring 1999

"Black Heaven" was published in MARYLAND REVIEW, #7, spring-fall 1995

TABLE OF CONTENTS

PASSAGE OF NO RETURN 1
BASTARD 2
TWO RIVERS 5
DAKAR BY DAY 6
SO MANY THINGS DIVIDE US 9
AUTHENTIC AFRICAN 10
HARLEM HOSPITAL WAITING ROOM 15
BLACK HEAVEN 17
PLEA FOR MALCOLM X 18
THE FORGOTTEN 21
PORT MARIA 24
RUNAWAYS 27
PAULA 28
I WAS BROWN, THEY WERE BLACK 33
THE WAR IS OVER 34
LOST MEMORY 37
JOSEPHINE BAKER AT FISK UNIVERSITY 38
RED SOUTH 41
TANNER'S "BANJO LESSON" 42
FOREIGNER 47
IN SWEDEN 48
AFRICAN MUSEUM 51
RESTLESS 52

I

Ooman
Homeland

PASSAGE OF NO RETURN

Black dungeon,
the smell of feces still alive.
The floor sloping down so urine could drain.
Above us, a castle painted white
and cool ocean spray.
Palm trees along the beach bend
their hands in prayer.

Rain splashed down thirty feet
from three square pockets
where daylight leaked in,
just enough to see each other's eyes—
chained bodies kept alive by memories.

As I emerge, I see
new smoke curl from nearby homes.
I hear drums beating.
In Cape Coast village
tribal chiefs and queen mothers
dressed in togas
sway in sedans above a crowd.

BASTARD

On Goree Island near Dakar,
I walked with my guide, Mustafa,
who embraced his blackness.

When I gave his daughter a gift—
a tube of Avon skin softener—
he snatched it away
as though it were plagued.

With his eyes he said:
foreigners raped our women
then turned their children into slaves.

At the hotel
I lay on the beach
until my skin peeled,
the sun blinding me.

TWO RIVERS

Red sand, an ancient place,
where camel trains drift beyond reeds
along the Nile. Further down
the river becomes a swamp
near the mouth of the Mississippi.
Black slaves work
on a wharf between cotton
stacked stories high, waiting
to be shipped across the sea.

It seldom rains around the Nile,
the sun hazy as if always waking up
or falling back to sleep for hundreds
and thousands of years. Even now,
as I write, I still can see wraiths
hauling stones on barges
to build the pyramids
or trudging on steamboat planks
lifting their heavy bales.

DAKAR BY DAY

Along the sea on rainbow sand
bearing tides that once cooled lava.
It's morning still and fish markets open.
Families gather by whispering fires,
their wooden boats washed ashore.
I'm sitting near a graveyard.
Buzzards perch on stones
with names like Amadou and Diallo.
Toward the horizon,
a ferry boat disappears
going to Goree Island.
Dakar squats behind me,
now rising to its feet,
stretching from a graveyard
to a hill crowned with
luxury hotels.

SO MANY THINGS DIVIDE US

Kwaku speaks the Twi language
even though he's not an Ashanti,
and he knows English, too, for foreigners.
He lives in Accra but has never seen Kumasi,
one hundred miles away.
On the steps of the hotel
he hustles with other young men
selling bracelets and beads and tours of Ghana.
He tells me, "Stay away from Nigerians,"
and he doesn't trust the whites.
As we walk to Tema together,
where he once loaded ships on the docks,
I see he doesn't wear shoes.
By sunset he will have some.

AUTHENTIC AFRICAN

Because her two boys are thin
and her husband lies in bed
with malaria,
she tramps each morning
to Dakar six miles away.

Along Rue George Pompidou
near the old French naval yard,
she pounds a teakwood dowel
up and down, grinding meal
inside a bowl.

While she sings a Wolof work song
to the throb of drums
beaten by dead ancestors,
blue cloth
wraps around her body.

Bus loads of tourists pass her.
They stop and get out
and pay ten francs
to take her picture
on their smart phones.

II

Nyanka
Orphans

HARLEM HOSPITAL WAITING ROOM

Black faces line rows
as in holds of ships
that once carried human cargo.
Silent, slow,
all afternoon the boat moves.
It has lots of time
in this room without a clock,
save the one whose hands
some soul did not turn back
from daylight's saving.

We wait
for doctors to return,
stroking our chins to stay calm.
Soap operas keep us company
on the colored screen.

Behind me a man,
for two hours he doesn't move.
In front a woman
who reads the daily news.
To my left, children:
they laugh, dance, sleep.

Months, years seem to pass,
until my name is called, and I
disappear behind closed doors.

BLACK HEAVEN

It smells of urine everywhere, here
beneath the subway to black heaven.

My heaven, these dungeon walls, dirt-caked
and scattered glass my foot crunches.

I feel naked in heaven,
a nakedness that wants to fly or ride
on top number four train; here it comes
like steel buffalo heard stampeding.

In black heaven, there is a river running.
It lies inside double tracks, a muddy creek,
so brown, so deep, my Ganges;
it sleeps the night of centuries.

It grows hot, it grows cold,
now lava flowing out of control;
it's my ocean,
it's my heaven,
this river running through black heaven.

PLEA FOR MALCOLM X

Malcolm, we need you now
in this age of ignorance and desperation.
We've cut off our contact with Africa,
we've ruptured our unity and pride:

the war between brothers and sisters,
the clash of the old with the young,
and now a mounting wealth divide—
those who have and those who don't.

We kill ourselves for vengeance or money
while some get bullied by police.
Malcolm, you must lift us up,
for we have fallen behind.

Help us rise again.
Lift us so we can live.

THE FORGOTTEN

My father was a white man, my mother black.
Their marriage fell apart.
My foster parents, a college professor and his wife,
adopted me after my parents' divorce;
they already had two kids.
Soon their marriage broke up,
and I got another mom who I hated.
Once I beat her up for something she said.
After that, I ran away from home,
dropped out of school, got pregnant.
When my boyfriend found out about the abortion,
he punched me and kicked me out.
I had nowhere to go, no money.
I called a teacher I knew from high school
who took me in for awhile,
but now it's time to go—
back on the streets again.

III

Awooh
Birth

PORT MARIA

I can tell when a slave ship arrives—
a stench so foul it makes me shake.
A small dot stains the horizon.
Creaking toward me,
it slowly comes to port.
No drums, flutes, or ceremonies.
Only the lush hills of Jamaica.
Only the bay filled with sharks
waiting for some wretch to jump.
Soon I hear coughing and frantic voices,
a few women screaming in spurts.
When they stumble from the boat
they are nothing but bones,
their skin scraped off by the planks
they have lain on for weeks.
I and the other traders scramble,
leaving the sick ones to die on the beach.

RUNAWAYS

For two days we don't eat
or talk to anyone
in this wagon that carries us
hiding under a pile of firewood.
But we hold each other
and count bumps on the road,
measuring the distance we come
and towns we passed.
It's turned April but snow still falls.
On Sunday we made Smyrna in Kent County
and Jeff Williams' house in Camden.
As we crossed the Big Choptank River,
I thought about our children sold last year:
Henrietta, small and frail,
and Johnny, so quiet all the time.
We tried to find them many times.
Even in the North,
someone will know where they are.

PAULA

It was the first time I saw someone
drown in their own blood,
my best friend shot in front of me,
but I survived if you can all it that
drinking water from the toilet
beaten at night by guards.

Like many young girls I resisted Batista
believing he had turned Cuba
into a playground for gangsters.
They transferred me to a women's jail
when I faked mental illness:
"here comes that crazy mulatto girl."

In '59 the bearded ones freed me.
I saw the man who killed my friend
after his capture at the Bay of Pigs
and later was put on trial.
What happened to him I won't say.
It's too terrible to talk about.

IV

Nkaeeh
Memory

I WAS BROWN, THEY WERE BLACK

When the white kids threw corn
at Marvin and Rayetta Jones
on the school bus
in the morning,
I sat by the window and asked,
    "Why should I intervene?"
Didn't they tell me,
    "You're different. You're one of us."
I lived on the right side of town,
    the Joneses lived by the meadow
I went shopping at the supermarket,
    they slaughtered pigs for meals.
I read books for white boys,
    they did what they had to do.
Corn flew wildly in the aisle.
Marvin held his sister's hand
flinging the grains back.

THE WAR IS OVER

I saw hundreds . . . of battle flags . . .
Borne through the smoke of the battle
                              —Walt Whitman

The wind blows across Charleston,
but you hang limp below the clouds.
Who will stop and look at you?
Who will fight for you now?

Confederates still salute you,
but what about the slaves
left rotting in the rice fields?
Should they pledge their allegiance?

I want to lower you,
to leave you in the past.
I want to think about what is
and what's to come.

LOST MEMORY

In my grandfather's basement
I once found a memoir signed
by Booker T. Washington,
its pages sliced and torn,
brown stains that looked
like old blood. It smelled of
darkness and muddy water,
clay floors, rivers, swamps.

So I asked my grandfather
to go back as far as he could.
What did he witness?
What did he endure?
For a moment his eyes stopped.
They had a glazed look,
staring in the void.

JOSEPHINE BAKER AT FISK UNIVERSITY

I know what you're thinking
that I abandoned you here in Nashville
to fight this Dixie town by yourselves.
Yeah, you think I ran away
to enjoy the fast life of a celebrity
banana dancing in Paris nightclubs
with Hemingway.

But you haven't heard the full story,
how I fled with mama to cross the Eads Bridge
just before a white mob torched East Saint Louis.
Goering tried to poison me during the war,
and I dodged Nazi bullets in North Africa.
When I came back to the States, I faced the color line:
thirty-six hotels turned me down, all the grand ones.
 "Sorry," they said, "we made a mistake."

RED SOUTH

Red is the color of clay in Atlanta
whose streets lie paved
with red dust blown from far away.
I have never lived in Georgia;
I have never known the South,
which I imagine is a distant land
of red shallow graves and rivers
swollen with dead Negroes.

Red is the color of one day in Kentucky
a bus driver screamed at me for no reason.
I thought right away his red eyes and veins
looked like those of lynchers
stringing up a black man above a fire,
its red flames rising wave upon wave.

TANNER'S "BANJO LESSON"
(after a painting by Henry O. Tanner)

An old black man bends his gaze
beyond his banjo
eyes that have known trembling waters
watched harsh suns go down
nose that sniffed fresh smoke
on the ridge of his youth
lips that kissed
hands that touched dusk
in North Carolina Hills.

A black boy, older than his years,
stands between knees of the man
on strings his fingers
flame, pulse, throb
the old man's banjo
as he strokes
the cave like room ignites
in song.

They are not players in a minstrel show
they do not wear the mask
they are tight as the strings they sow
notes that pull mountains, earth
let the sorrow songs carry them home

v

Ohmanfrani
Foreigner

FOREIGNER

As I lie on the bank looking
across the Thames, a sign reads
"Greater London Council
is working for you."
Yesterday at the Y.M.C.A.,
I changed my room to a smaller one
on the fourth floor,
where I met my neighbor Sam, from Kenya.
He said when a group of Africans
travel on the bus
by the end of the trip
they know each other.
"But here sometimes no one talks at all."
Later, we went out to a nightclub
for beer. In the dark corner
a group of women laughed
among themselves.
When he asked one to dance
she told him no.
He grew sullen after that
as we walked home.

IN SWEDEN

We had just left Marsta
when we passed
underneath a bridge,
large letters scrawled in white:

NO NIGGERS.

I sat up in my seat,
the train speeding
towards Sweden's ancient capital.
My knuckles bent into fists.
Even here I could not escape
the color of my skin.

In the afternoon,
I climbed the hill that led to the castle,
where Queen Christina quit the throne
because she did not love war.
Now children played among
the rusting cannons.
When I came down
at the end of the day,
I stopped in a café to rest.
Through the windows
I watched a black man
helping a blind man
who didn't seem to mind,
nor did the people who crossed the street.

AFRICAN MUSEUM

The tram took me there,
through thick woods
that blocked the sun.
I got off at Tervuren,
the last stop.
Rising from nowhere,
I saw a palace with
titanic walls, columns,
fountains and pools,
gardens farther than I could see.

Inside, stuffed crocodiles,
monkeys, gorillas with sad eyes.
Even a stuffed giraffe.
Butterflies the size of my chest
lay under glass.
Pieces of broken rocks:
cataloged.

Stuffed soldiers stood with bayonets,
stuffed explorers posed.

Afterwards, I rode the tram
past the dark forest
towards Brussels.

RESTLESS

At Euston Station, yesterday,
I talked to a Nigerian student
dressed in a suit and tie.
He kept repeating that
the problems of the world
stem from greed.
He was right, but I
could not respond.
So I left and drifted down
Tottenham Court Road
by late afternoon.

Youths lay in London's streets:
skinheads, punks,
Rastafarians with dreadlocks;
more homeless people,
more police.

Then it began to rain, gently
after the sun went down
and lingering past midnight
when daybreak began again.

Robert Coles, both educator and poet, began his career in 1972 teaching African Literature at Temple University in Pennsylvania. He earned a PhD in American Literature from the State University of New York at Buffalo in 1979. He went on to teach at Howard University, Fordham University, and Berea College. In 1989 he joined the faculty at Hampshire College in Massachusetts where he also taught African Literature and Prison Literature before retiring in 2009 to pursue writing full-time. In 1999 he published a monograph titled, *Black Writers Abroad*. During the late 1990s and early 2000s Coles began research on the life and work of African Russian poet Alexander Pushkin. His memoir, *Pursuing Alexander Pushkin* was published in 2024. He has also written a film biopic about Alexander Pushkin, which has already won numerous screenplay awards. Coles has published over one hundred poems in periodicals, magazines, and anthologies since 1983. His chapbook *Personalities* was published by Moonstone Arts Center in 2024.

www.ingramcontent.com/pod-product-compliance
Lightning Source LLC
LaVergne TN
LVHW051201080426
835508LV00021B/2750